KenArnoldBooks   www.kenarnoldbooks.com

David Hill offers quirky perspectives on life, love, and globalization in his first book of poems to be published in the United States. A journalist whose normal beat is international economy and culture, Hill is known to readers of his poetry as, in the words of *Light Quarterly* (Chicago), "a polylingual perversely talented poet, [who] does devilishly contrived things with the language. He's raunchy, unsolemn, and very funny."

"David Hill makes the everyday surreal—and writes unashamedly and delightfully about love. Imagine a shape-shifter, a spinner of yarns, a poet from Transylvania via the U.S. and leafy England, whose poems are small gothic tales of lost dogs, lovesick girls, royal houses gone to pot, celebrities in domestic situation comedies, vampires in the belfry, menopausal women and much more."

—*Rosemary Dun*, founder and host, *Big Mouth Poetry*

"Long an admirer, I had been prepared to be amused by David Hill's new collection of poems. I was not quite prepared for how astonishingly good they are. He is also well on his way to becoming a major poet—perhaps the first for the era of globalization."

—*James Bowman*, former American editor, the *Times Literary Supplement*

David Hill has written for nonfiction books published by Blue Guides, Oxford Business Group, and the Stockholm Network—and contributed to news products from the *Financial Times* and *Economist* groups. As a poet, he is published in more than twenty anthologies. A debut collection was issued in 1999 by the U.K.'s National Poetry Foundation. He has also written and translated lyrics for recording artists, and words for stage and screen.

KenArnoldBooks LLC
Cover photograph by Kimberli Ransom.
Cover and interior design by Tomaso Milian

ISBN: 978-0-9799634-6-9

9 780979 963469   51400

"Inflation might almost be called legal counter-feiting."

— Economist Irving Fisher
STABILIZING THE DOLLAR, 1920

"The power of taxation by currency depreciation is one which has been inherent in the State since Rome discovered it."

— Economist John Maynard Keynes
"Social Consequences of Changes
in the Value of Money"
in ESSAYS IN PERSUASION, 1933

About the "Uncle Eric" Series

The "Uncle Eric" series of books is written by Richard J. Maybury for young and old alike. Using the epistolary style of writing (using letters to tell a story), Mr. Maybury plays the part of an economist writing a series of letters to his niece or nephew. Using stories and examples, he gives interesting and clear explanations of topics that are generally thought to be too difficult for anyone but experts.

Mr. Maybury warns, "beware of anyone who tells you a topic is above you or better left to experts. Many people are twice as smart as they think they are but they've been intimidated into believing some topics are above them. You can understand almost anything if it is explained well."

The series is called UNCLE ERIC'S MODEL OF HOW THE WORLD WORKS (For a full explanation see pages 5-9 of this book). Each book in the series attempts to be consistent with the principles of America's Founders. The books can be read in any order, and have been written to stand alone. To get the most from each one, however, Mr. Maybury suggests the following order of reading.

Uncle Eric's Model
of How the World Works

Uncle Eric Talks About Personal, Career and Financial Security

Whatever Happened to Penny Candy?

Whatever Happened to Justice?

Are You Liberal? Conservative? or Confused?

Ancient Rome: How It Affects You Today

Evaluating Books: What Would Thomas Jefferson Think About This?

The Money Mystery

The Clipper Ship Strategy

The Thousand Year War

(Study guides available or forthcoming for above titles.)

An "Uncle Eric" Book

The
Money Mystery

*The hidden force affecting your career,
business and investments*

First sequel to WHATEVER HAPPENED TO PENNY CANDY?

by Richard J. Maybury
("Uncle Eric")

published by
Bluestocking Press
P.O. Box 1014 • Dept. MM
Placerville • CA • 95667-1014

Printed and bound in the United States of America.

Cover illustration by Bob O'Hara, Georgetown, CA.
Edited by Jane A. Williams.

Library of Congress Cataloging-in-Publication Data
Maybury, Rick.
    The money mystery : the hidden force affecting your career, business and investments / by Richard J. Maybury.
        p. cm. -- (An "Uncle Eric" book)
    Includes bibliographical references and index.
    ISBN 0-942617-27-4 (alk. paper)
    1. Money. 2. Monetary policy. 3. Financial security. I. Title
II. Series: Maybury, Rick. "Uncle Eric" book.
HG221.M125 1997
332.4--DC21   97-18712
                                               CIP

Published by   **Bluestocking Press**
                  Post Office Box 1014
                     Dept. MM
                Placerville, CA 95667-1014

To the center of my life,
Marilyn

Uncle Eric's Model
of How the World Works

What is a model? In his book UNCLE ERIC TALKS ABOUT PERSONAL, CAREER AND FINANCIAL SECURITY, Richard Maybury (Uncle Eric) explains that one of the most important things you can teach children, or learn yourself, is:

"Models are how we think, they are how we understand how the world works. As we go through life we build these very complex pictures in our minds of how the world works, and we're constantly referring back to them—matching incoming data against our models. That's how we make sense of things. One of the most important uses for models is in sorting incoming information to decide if it's important or not.

"In most schools, models are never mentioned because the teachers are unaware of them. One of the most dangerous weaknesses in traditional education is that it contains no model for political history. Teachers teach what they were taught — and no one ever mentioned models to them, so they don't teach them to their students. For the most part, children are just loaded down with collections of facts that they are made to memorize. Without good models, children have no way to know which facts are important and which are not. Students leave school thinking history is a senseless waste of time. Then, deprived of the real lessons of history, the student is vulnerable."

The question is, which models to teach. Mr. Maybury says, "the two models that I think are crucially important for everyone to learn are economics and law."

WHATEVER HAPPENED TO PENNY CANDY? explains the economic model, which is based on Austrian economics, the most free-market of all economic models. WHATEVER HAPPENED TO JUSTICE? explains the legal model, and shows the connection between rational law and economic progress. The legal model is the old British Common Law — or Natural Law. The original principles on which America was founded were those of the old British Common Law.

These two books, PENNY CANDY and JUSTICE, provide the overall model of how human civilization works, especially the world of money.

Once the model is understood, read ARE YOU LIBERAL? CONSERVATIVE? OR CONFUSED? which explains political philosophies relative to Uncle Eric's Model — and makes a strong case for consistency to that model, no exceptions.

Next, read ANCIENT ROME: HOW IT AFFECTS YOU TODAY which shows what happens when a society ignores Uncle Eric's Model and embraces fascism.

To help you locate books and authors generally in agreement with these economic and legal models, Mr. Maybury wrote EVALUATING BOOKS: WHAT WOULD THOMAS JEFFERSON THINK ABOUT THIS? which provides guidelines for selecting books that are consistent with the principles of America's founders. You can apply these guidelines to books, movies, news commentators, current events — to any spoken or written medium.

Further expanding on the economic model is THE MONEY MYSTERY which explains the hidden force affecting your career, business and investments. Some economists refer to this force as velocity, others to the demand for money. Whichever term is used, it is one of the least understood forces affecting your life. Knowing about velocity and the demand for money not only gives you an understanding of history that few others have, it prepares you to understand and avoid pitfalls in your career, business and investments. THE MONEY MYSTERY is the first sequel to WHATEVER HAPPENED TO PENNY CANDY? and provides essential background for getting the most from THE CLIPPER SHIP STRATEGY.

THE CLIPPER SHIP STRATEGY explains how government's interference in the economy affects business, careers and investments. It's a practical nuts-and-bolts strategy for prospering in our turbulent economy. This book is the second sequel to WHATEVER HAPPENED TO PENNY CANDY? and should be read after THE MONEY MYSTERY.

Soon to be available is THE THOUSAND YEAR WAR: THE LITTLE UNDERSTOOD MID-EAST CONFLICT AND HOW IT AFFECTS YOU TODAY. In the 1970s, '80s and '90s, the thousand year war has been the cause of the greatest shocks to the investment markets — the oil embargoes, the Iranian hostage crisis, and the Iraq-Kuwait war — and it is likely to remain so for decades to come. Forewarned is forearmed. You must understand where this war is leading to manage your career, business and investments.

These books can be read in any order and have been written to stand alone. But to get the most from each one, Mr. Maybury suggests the following order of reading:

Uncle Eric's Model
of How the World Works

Book 1. UNCLE ERIC TALKS ABOUT PERSONAL, CAREER AND
FINANCIAL SECURITY.
Uncle Eric's Model introduced.

Book 2. WHATEVER HAPPENED TO PENNY CANDY? *A Fast, Clear
and Fun Explanation of the Economics You Need for
Success in Your Career, Business and Investments.*
The economic model explained. The clearest most
interesting explanation of economics around.

Book 3. WHATEVER HAPPENED TO JUSTICE?
The legal model explained. Explores America's
legal heritage. Discusses the difference between
higher law and man-made law, and the connection
between rational law and economic prosperity.

Book 4. ARE YOU LIBERAL? CONSERVATIVE? OR CONFUSED?
Political labels. What do they mean? Liberal,
conservative, left, right, democrat, republican, moderate, socialist, libertarian, communist—what are
their economic policies and what plans do their
promoters have for your money? Clear, concise
explanations. Facts and fallacies. The model applied and misapplied.

Book 5. ANCIENT ROME: *How It Affects You Today.*
The model ignored. Are we heading for fascism like
ancient Rome? Mr. Maybury uses historical events
to explain current events. Take a look at ancient
Roman government and how it affects you today.

Book 6. EVALUATING BOOKS: *What Would Thomas Jefferson Think About This?* Learn how to identify the philosophical slant of most writers and media commentators on the subjects of law, history, economics, and literature.

Book 7. THE MONEY MYSTERY: *The Hidden Force Affecting Your Career, Business and Investments.* Some economists refer to velocity, others to the demand for money. However it is seen, it is one of the least understood forces affecting our businesses, careers and investments. The first sequel to WHATEVER HAPPENED TO PENNY CANDY?, THE MONEY MYSTERY prepares you to understand and avoid pitfalls in your career, business and investments.

Book 8. THE CLIPPER SHIP STRATEGY: *For Success in Your Career, Business and Investments.* Practical nuts-and-bolts strategy for prospering in our turbulent economy, CLIPPER SHIP STRATEGY is the second sequel to WHATEVER HAPPENED TO PENNY CANDY? and should be read after THE MONEY MYSTERY.

Book 9: THE THOUSAND YEAR WAR: *The Little Understood Mid-East Conflict and How It Affects You Today.* Forthcoming Title. In the 1970s, '80s and '90s, the thousand year war has been the cause of the greatest shocks to the investment markets — the oil embargoes, the Iranian hostage crisis, and the Iraq-Kuwait war — and it is likely to remain so for decades to come. Forewarned is forearmed. You must understand where this war is leading to manage your career, business and investments.

Quantity Discounts Available

This book, and all other books in the "Uncle Eric" series, are available at special quantity discounts for bulk purchases to individuals, businesses, schools, libraries, and associations, to be distributed as gifts, premiums, or as fund raisers.

For terms and discount schedule contact:

Marketing Department
Bluestocking Press
P.O. Box 1014
Dept. MM
Placerville, CA 95667-1014
Phone: 800-959-8586; 916-621-1123
Fax: 916-642-9222

Specify how books are to be distributed: as gifts, premiums, fund raisers — or to be resold.

Contents

Note to Reader

Throughout each "Uncle Eric" book, whenever a word that appears in the glossary is introduced in the text, it is displayed in a **bold typeface.**

Author's Disclosure

For reasons I do not understand, writers today are supposed to be objective. Few disclose the viewpoints or opinions they use to decide what information is important and what is not, or what shall be presented or omitted.

I do not adhere to this standard and make no pretense of being objective. I am biased in favor of liberty, free markets and international neutrality, and proud of it. So, I disclose my viewpoint which you will find explained in detail in my newsletter and my other books.[1]

For those who have not yet read these publications, I call my viewpoint Juris Naturalism (pronounced *jur*-es *nach*-e-re-liz-em, sometimes abbreviated JN) meaning the belief in a natural law that is higher than any government's law. Here are six quotes from America's founders that help to describe this viewpoint:

"...all men are created equal, that they are endowed by their Creator with certain unalienable rights."
— Declaration of Independence, 1776

"The natural rights of the colonists are these: first, a right to life; second to liberty; third to property; together with the right to support and defend them in the best manner they can."
— Samuel Adams, 1772

---

[1] See RICHARD MAYBURY'S EARLY WARNING REPORT newsletter, published by Henry-Madison Research, Box 1616-V, Rocklin, CA, 95677, and his books (see pgs. 6-10), published by Bluestocking Press, P.O. Box 1014, Placerville, CA, 95667.

"It is strangely absurd to suppose that a million of human beings collected together are not under the same moral laws which bind each of them separately."
— Thomas Jefferson, 1816

"A wise and frugal government, which shall restrain men from injuring one another, which shall leave them otherwise free to regulate their own pursuits of industry and improvement, and shall not take from the mouth of labor the bread it has earned. This is the sum of good government."
— Thomas Jefferson, 1801

"Not a place on earth might be so happy as America. Her situation is remote from all the wrangling world, and she has nothing to do but to trade with them."
— Thomas Paine, 1776

"The great rule of conduct for us, in regard to foreign nations, is, in extending our commercial relations, to have with them as little political connection as possible."
— George Washington, 1796

George
Washington

Fable of the Frog

Once upon a time there was a frog who noticed his fellow frogs were being devoured by a snake. He fearfully went to a wise old owl and asked what to do. The owl said, "When the snake comes near, fly away." The frog thanked the owl for this sage advice and confidently hopped away.

A few days later the snake came. As the frog was disappearing down the snake's throat, he heard the owl say, "Sorry, I only deal with theory, not reality."

1

The Financial Panic of 1980

Dear Chris,

It was good hearing from you. I am not surprised that after studying the 1980s in your history class, you are still confused about the economic events of that decade. Your observations are correct, for the most part history books report political history, and ignore economic history. Without the economic side, historical events seldom make much sense. I am glad you wrote me, I'll try to help complete the picture for you.

You said you want to understand why economic times in the 1980s were so tough for so many people, including your Mom and Dad.

Your parents have given me permission to discuss the roller coaster economic events that affected their lives. They were surprised to know it had such an effect on you, since you were so young at the time. But on reflection, they remember the many stories their own parents, your grandparents, told about the Great Depression of the 1930s.

Your parents want to do everything they can to help you be better prepared than they were to handle whatever comes your way.

To discuss the 1980s with a clear picture, however, we must go back at least to 1970, for the 1980s were the result of earlier events. We will look at the whole period from 1970 to 1990, as well as some events from the more distant past.

Chris, before we get started, you should review our prior correspondence about **economics**.[2] Pay particular attention to letters seven and eight to refresh your knowledge of **business cycles**, and the terms **money supply, velocity** and **the demand for money**. It will only take a few minutes and will make what I am about to explain in my next few letters easier to understand, since what's to come will be a continuation of our prior discussion.

I'll write again in a couple of days, after you have had time to dig out those letters and review them. In my next letter, I'll talk about the government's manipulation of the economy, meaning its manipulation of your career, business and investments. Then we will look at the financial panic of 1980, and the causes and ramifications of this panic.

I will finish this set of letters by discussing the short-term outlook you must adopt to cope with the new economic environment spawned by the 1980 panic.

Uncle Eric

---

[2] See WHATEVER HAPPENED TO PENNY CANDY? by Richard Maybury, published by Bluestocking Press, Placerville, CA.

2

A Shot of Inflation

Dear Chris,

Do you think the government manipulates our livelihoods as if we were puppets on a string?

Do you have any evidence to support your opinion?

Here are a few paragraphs from a news story that appeared in early 1986:

> "In recent weeks the White House has made it clear that **Fed [Federal Reserve System]** Chairman Paul Volcker must march more to its tune in this critical congressional-election year....
>
> "The President and some key advisers want Volcker poised to push easy **money** if the economy appears weak....
>
> "Explains Washington insider Robert Strauss: 'Volcker is a great chairman. Unfortunately, some areas of the country that want a shot of **inflation** will influence decision making this year. Volcker can't resist it.' "[3]

---

[3] "Economic Outlook," U.S. NEWS & WORLD REPORT, April 7, 1986, p. 64.

The use of monetary policy to "fine tune" the business cycle — meaning to fine tune our livelihoods — and thereby influence elections is an ancient art. Here is another news blurb, from August 2, 1982:

"Before the Federal Reserve Board reduced its discount rate, at least two top White House aides bluntly told Chairman Paul Volcker that President Reagan wanted to see faster expansion of the money supply to cut interest rates and boost economic recovery before election day."[4]

This one appeared a few weeks later:

"Many suspicious Democrats in Congress openly predict that the drop in interest rates won't last. Their scenario: The Federal Reserve Board will permit borrowing costs to decline only until after the November 2nd elections — to take Reagan and the Republicans off the hook."[5]

The suspicious democrats were right. Immediately after the 1982 elections, interest rates went into a two-year uptrend. This uptrend ended just before the 1984 elections.

As the two news blurbs show, business conditions are not manipulated for the benefit of the people, they are manipulated for the benefit of the government.

Does **political power** corrupt?

What do you think?

---

[4] Ibid., August 2, 1982, p. 16.
[5] Ibid., August 30, 1982, p. 11.

Ever since the creation of the Federal Reserve System in 1913, officials have been "adjusting" business conditions. Thousands of businesses, careers and investments have been mangled and twisted as easily as coat hanger wires, to fit the needs of each successive administration.

Officials thought they could do this forever, but they were wrong. By 1980, metal fatigue had set in and the wires were in danger of breaking. The panic of 1980 was a warning.

I will explain this warning shortly, but first I need to say a few words about the fact that government officials never discuss this warning, they are too busy generating misleading propaganda. It is this misleading propaganda that trapped your parents and a lot of other innocent people.

Uncle Eric

P.S. Chris, the reason I write these letters is to give you a viewpoint you won't get anywhere else. Few people talk about what's *really* happening when government officials change their laws and policies. If you don't get this side of the story from me you will probably never get it at all.

3

Misleading Propaganda

Dear Chris,

Throughout most of the 1980's, officials praised the economic recovery. Ecstatic that the 1982 recession had ended, they boasted about their astute handling of economic policy.

In 1983 and 1984 many employers assumed these official pronouncements about the recovery were true and they began expanding. Your Dad was one of them. He invested heavily in a new office building, computers and hired more workers. Employers bet heavily that the recovery was real.

The superstar of high tech, Apple Computer, launched its new Macintosh line of personal computers. But sales of the new miracle PC did not achieve expectations and in June 1985 Apple announced the closing of three of its six plants and layoffs of 1200 workers. Its stock fell to $14.62 from a January high of $30. This at a time when the so-called recovery was roaring.

By the end of the decade the truth about the recovery was widely known. The Reagan era boom had not been nationwide, it had been confined to certain areas, notably the stock market and the two coasts; much between the two coasts was still hurting.

Why was it confined to the stock market and the coasts? It has something to do with a process economists call the **injection effect.** It's too complex to explain in this set of letters, but I promise I'll cover it in a future set.[6] Our subject for now is the little known forces of velocity and the demand for money. To continue...

Houston and Denver were in **depressions.** U.S. car sales remained below the levels of the early 1970s.[7] The banking system was a mess — the rescue of the Savings & Loans would cost more than $100 billion. The oil industry was still distressed. Farmers were nowhere near as well off as they had been in the previous decade. The 1987 crash had decimated Wall Street's financial firms.

Perhaps the most important but least publicized story was the growing hardship of the young. The "real" (inflation-adjusted) average income of families headed by persons under age 30 (which included your parents) had plunged 14 percent.[8] Persons over age 40 were doing wonderfully but poverty among the under-30 generation had nearly doubled.[9]

The American economy had been severely damaged at the start of the decade, before Mr. Reagan came to power, and by the end of the decade it was still damaged. There had been no real recovery.

What happened? We cannot be sure, economics is not an exact science, but studies show the velocity of circulation of the dollar had become erratic and gone into decline. Each

---

[6] See THE CLIPPER SHIP STRATEGY by Richard Maybury, published by Bluestocking Press.

[7] THE ECONOMIST, April 1, 1989, p. 62.

[8] "America's Income Gap, The Closer You Look, The Worse It Gets," BUSINESS WEEK, April 17, 1989, p. 78.

[9] Ibid.

time the Federal Reserve injected money into the economy to spark a recovery, the injection was offset by a fall in velocity — a repeat of the experience of the 1930's Great Depression.

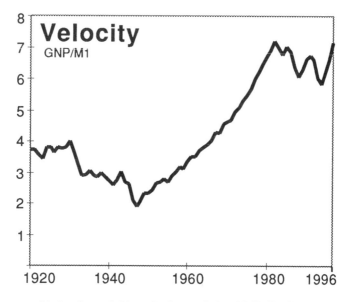

Velocity of Circulation of the U.S. Dollar

Velocity is the speed at which dollars change hands. It is a measure of the demand for money, which is the willingness of people to hold dollars.

When velocity is high, people are trading their dollars away quickly, which means the demand for dollars is low.

When velocity is low, people are trading their dollars away slowly, which means the demand for dollars is high.

Velocity was in a stable rising trend for 35 years after World War II. The financial panic of 1980 broke this trend, and velocity has remained unstable ever since.

This has left federal officials with a major problem. How do they know what the supply of dollars should be when they do not know what the demand for dollars will be?

The news media reported almost none of this because so few Americans knew enough economics to understand. In fact, I doubt many reporters or editors understood. (Most still don't.) But the Federal Reserve's economists discussed it incessantly in the Fed's publications. For a small sample of these discussions read:

• "Money & Velocity In The 1980s" by John B. Carlson and John N. McElraveny, ECONOMIC COMMENTARY, Federal Reserve Bank of Cleveland, January 15, 1989.

• "Solving the 1980s' Velocity Puzzle: A Progress Report," by Courtenay C. Stone & Daniel L. Thornton, REVIEW, Federal Reserve Bank of St. Louis, August 1987.

• "Money Demand — Some Long Run Properties," QUARTERLY REVIEW, Federal Reserve Bank of New York, Spring 1988.

• "Monetarism and the M1 Target," by William T. Gavin, ECONOMIC COMMENTARY, Federal Reserve Bank of Cleveland, October 1, 1986.

These are complex, scholarly articles written for economists, but if you want to get into the subject deeply, you might try them. Unfortunately, I don't know of anything about velocity and money demand that's written on a level most people could understand. This is why I write you these letters.

You can see from the chart that after World War II, velocity went into a stable uptrend for 35 years. This stability ended in 1980, and as far as we know has never returned.

Clearly, something dramatic happened to velocity and the demand for money in the U.S. To understand it we need to learn a bit more about velocity and the financial panic of 1980. Then we will look at the great crash of 1987, and the meaning of all this for our future.

Uncle Eric

4

The French Example

Dear Chris,

To understand the velocity puzzle today it helps to study a historical parallel. True stories are easier to understand than mathematical models. And, history is often repeated.

The following description of velocity in action during the great French **runaway inflation** is taken from Andrew Dickson White's fine book FIAT MONEY INFLATION IN FRANCE published and presented to members of the U.S. House and Senate in 1876.

In 1790 the French government was running short of cash and searching for a new way to finance its spending. Fearful of a tax rebellion, the politicians hit on a bold new plan to pay for everything they were buying. They began printing money.

This plan was popular, it enabled the French government to pay its debts and engage in all kinds of new activities without burdening the people with higher taxes.

The **paper money** was called the **assignat** (English pronunciation ass-ig-nat) and when it was first issued it was widely accepted. But this first stage of the inflation lasted only a few months. Each time a new wave of assignats was injected into the economy, the value of each individual assignat fell. Prices rose to compensate for the assignat's fall in value.

In my previous set of letters[10] we covered the three stages of inflation. In the **first stage**, prices do not rise as fast as the money supply does because people don't know what is happening. Some delay their spending in hopes prices will fall back. In effect, they take some of the money out of circulation as the government is pumping it in. That was France in 1790.

In the **second stage**, many people have caught on, and are spending their money quickly. Prices rise faster than the money supply because each unit of the money is changing hands faster. Many people want to get rid of it quickly and are willing to accept less for it.

In the **third stage**, the runaway, the whole population is in a panic to get rid of the money as soon as they get their hands on it, and the money declines to its real value, which is the value of scrap paper.

In 1790 France, the first stage of assignat inflation quickly gave way to the second stage, as people began to get wise to what was happening. Knowing their paper money was losing value, they would not save it. Each time a person received an assignat, he would rush out and spend it before its value could fall further. Demand for the assignat weakened and velocity increased.

The merchants accepting the assignats knew the value of the money was falling and they needed some way to protect themselves against the risks of accepting it. Some decided to

---

[10] See WHATEVER HAPPENED TO PENNY CANDY? by Richard Maybury, published by Bluestocking Press, Placerville, CA.

avoid the risk altogether by trading their goods or services only for gold or silver, which they knew the government could not create on a printing press.

Others continued accepting paper money but with a difference. Mr. White explained that in setting prices, "the merchant was forced to add to his ordinary profit a sum sufficient to cover probable or possible fluctuations in value." To pay the higher prices demanded by its suppliers, the government printed more paper money. Like a dog chasing its tail, the inflation grew worse. The demand for money kept falling and velocity kept increasing.

By 1793, an item that cost 25 assignats in 1790 had risen to 1000 assignats. A mere six months later it had risen to 7000.

The demand for the assignat was falling like a rock as, in White's words, "everyone endeavors to invest his doubtful paper in buildings, machines, and goods, which, under all circumstances, retain some intrinsic value."

A full blown stage three inflation was fast developing and the politicians were becoming desperate. To stop the decline in demand for the assignat they enacted wage and price controls. These controls forbade anyone to sell goods or services above certain stated prices. They also forbade any trade in gold, silver or foreign currencies; the penalty for breaking these laws was a stiff fine.

So, a **black market**[11] developed. People began spending their assignats covertly, in order to get rid of them as fast as possible.

The politicians decided the solution to this problem was to put more teeth into the law. The fine was increased.

---

[11] A black market is the production, sale or trade of goods or services against the wishes of the government.

This had little effect, so even more teeth were added. Anyone caught trading with gold, silver or foreign currencies was sentenced to six years in prison. A second offense was twenty years.

Still the black market flourished. Demand for the assignat continued falling and prices rising. Soap sellers in Paris had to add so much cushion into their prices to protect against the declining value of the paper money that washerwomen could hardly afford to purchase soap. In danger of losing their ability to earn their livings, mobs of angry washerwomen demanded that anyone who sold soap at high prices be punished with death. Yes, death. A runaway inflation can do terrible things to people. It can turn them into a mob.

On February 28, 1793, a riot swept Paris. Mobs of men and women went from bakery to bakery stealing bread — it was too expensive for them to buy. When the bread ran out, they began stealing rice and sugar, and then anything else they could carry away.

The French politicians were becoming more desperate to stop the declining demand for assignats. In May 1793, they took the final step, declaring the death penalty for any person convicted of "having asked, before a bargain was concluded, in what money payment was to be made."

To keep their desperate countrymen from fleeing the chaos, they also declared the death penalty for any Frenchman caught investing in a foreign country.

These brutal measures worked to some extent. The inflation cooled a bit, for a while; stage three was reduced to stage two. But the respite was only temporary and by 1795 the inflation was again solidly into stage three. Despite the price controls, a measure of flour that cost two assignats in 1790 was now at 225.

Debtors were ecstatic. Anyone who had borrowed 10,000 assignats in 1790 could repay the debt with the equivalent of 35 assignats.

Finally the desperate French politicians decided to scrap the assignat and replace it with a new currency, the **mandat**. But the mandat turned out to be an even worse failure than the assignat. The French people had learned their lesson about paper money, and demand for the mandat began to soften even before the new currency was off the presses.

For the mandat there was no stage one. As the new money entered the economy it entered already in stage two. The first mandats were accepted at only 35 percent of their face value. This quickly fell to 15 percent, and within six months the mandat was in stage three, trading at only three percent of its face value.

The fines and imprisonment designed to prop up the demand for the assignat were revived for the mandat. Anyone who was overheard speaking as little as a single word against the mandat could be placed in irons for four years.

But nothing worked and velocity continued to soar. By May 1797 the demand for paper money had sunk to zero. No one would accept it in trade for anything; it was worthless.

Deprived of a reliable currency for conducting trade, the French economy was a shambles. Unemployment, fear and hunger stalked the land.

Finally in 1799 there was a **coup d' etat** in which the government was overthrown and replaced by a strong, ruthless **dictator** — a man of action. He vowed that as long as he lived he would never again permit the French government to issue paper money. His name was Napoleon Bonaparte and his lust for political power threw Europe into one of the worst orgies of bloodshed ever known.

The French example demonstrates that when it comes to producing desperation, chaos and war, few things work as well as paper money.

The point to remember is that there is nothing to keep any of this from happening again in the U.S. — in the whole world — at any time. In 1979-80 it nearly did.

"That paper money has some advantages, is admitted. But that its abuses also are inevitable, and, by breaking up the measure of value, makes a lottery of all private property, cannot be denied. Shall we ever be able to put a constitutional veto on it?"

— Thomas Jefferson, 1817

Uncle Eric

5

Stage Two Inflation

Dear Chris,

In 1976, James Earl Carter was elected president largely on the assumption he would end the corruption that grew during the Nixon years.

The new Carter administration immediately began printing dollars to finance its spending.

During the first two years of Mr. Carter's reign, the number of dollars in the U.S. economy increased by 55 billion, or 18 percent. This rapid inflation of the money supply did not escape the notice of foreign holders of dollars, and these people began dumping their dollars in favor of assets which could not be created out of thin air — gold and silver.

At the time of Mr. Carter's election, gold was about $100 per ounce. A year later investors were getting nervous and gold hit $150. A year after that they were even more nervous and gold hit $200.

Mr. Carter's economic advisors said the demand for gold was nothing to worry about, expansion of the money supply could continue without danger. The "barbaric relic" (gold) was no longer important in world affairs, they said.

Unfortunately, the application was not quite so neat as the theory. In 1979, the barbaric relic was at $300 and rising, and the nation was clearly in a stage two inflation. The Carter administration finally realized it had better do something to stop the declining demand for the dollar. Investors worldwide were becoming frightened, there was serious danger the inflation would slip into stage three and velocity would soar, as it did in 1790s France.

As gold closed in on $400, Mr. Carter asked Paul Volcker to accept chairmanship of the Federal Reserve. Mr. Volcker did so, promising to restore confidence in the dollar.

October 6, 1979, brought an emergency meeting of the Federal Reserve Open Market Committee. The members unanimously agreed the Fed would no longer target interest rates, it would target money supply.

This meant the Fed would concentrate exclusively on keeping money supply growth within tightly defined boundaries, allowing interest rates to go wherever this might send them.

This new monetary policy was enacted in concert with a Treasury announcement that Treasury gold would no longer be sold at regularly scheduled intervals. Fort Knox would be slowly drained, at random times in random amounts. This, it was hoped, would throw a great deal of uncertainty into gold ownership and diminish the demand for gold.

The two actions had the desired effect. The demand for gold and silver stopped rising and the demand for the dollar appeared to be stabilizing — for a few weeks.

Uncle Eric

6

Khomeini

Dear Chris,

On November 3, 1979, followers of Ayatollah Khomeini seized the American embassy in Iran and took 52 hostages. They wanted the Shah.

In 1953, the U.S. Central Intelligence Agency had helped put the Shah in power. A ruthless dictator, he became a long-time ally and Mideast surrogate of U.S. officials. His secret police brutalized thousands of innocent people. The Iranian militants wanted to give him (and the U.S. government) a dose of his own medicine.

The Khomeini government could not or would not do anything about the hostages, and neither could the Carter administration. With the 1980 election campaigns approaching, the politicians were desperate to do something to end the crisis quickly.

Someone came up with the "brilliant" idea of freezing[12] Iranian assets in the U.S. The theory behind the **freeze** was simple: You have our people and we have your money, let's deal.

---

[12] Freezing means holding in place. In effect, this was a confiscation of Iranian assets.

But the application was not quite so neat as the theory. The militants holding the hostages were not wealthy Iranians who kept their money in America, so they were quite immune to the freeze. They wanted the Shah and this is all they wanted; they couldn't have cared less if the freeze lasted forever.

So, the money stayed frozen.[13] Mr. Carter could not release it because this would appear to the voters to be a capitulation. Week after week, both the money and the hostages remained imprisoned, with the world watching and waiting to see what would happen.

I should point out that a freeze is an extremely serious action normally taken only during a major war such as World War II. The reason is that millions of foreign investors keep their wealth in the form of dollars invested in America. They must not be frightened into dumping their dollars and fleeing America. If a freeze on one nation's assets occurs, they must be able to see quickly and clearly that the cause is so serious and unusual there is no danger of a freeze also happening to them.

But this was apparently not well understood by American officials. As the world watched and waited, other foreign investors began to wonder about the safety of their money. What might happen to my money, they asked, if my government does something to anger the American government? Will my money be frozen, too?

A **run** on the dollar began, first among wealthy Arabs whose governments were not on good terms with U.S. officials, then among wealthy persons worldwide. A panic

---

[13] In exchange for release of the hostages in 1981, U.S. officials gave back $3.89 billion, but at the end of the decade some $5 billion remained frozen. Source: U.S. NEWS & WORLD REPORT, August 28, 1989, p. 89.

developed to convert dollars into gold and other currencies and move them beyond the grasp of the U.S. government.

Demand for the dollar plunged as the Fed's October 6th rescue package was overwhelmed. Gold headed for $600 and the disintegration of the world economy began to look like a serious possibility. The more knowledgeable investors began to remember the great French runaway inflation.

Unfortunately, few people in the news media understood such concepts as velocity and the demand for money, so most did not understand what they were watching. They reported it, but the reports were so scattered and disjointed you could understand only if you knew what to look for.

The November 26, 1979, U.S. NEWS & WORLD REPORT contained two important statements. First, "The dollar is faltering. Foreign holders of dollars are tempted to move to another currency fearing their funds in the U.S. could also be blocked." Second, "The U.S. decision has aroused concern over the fate of Arab assets and investments in case of mounting political differences between the Arabs and the U.S."

The December 17, 1979, BUSINESS WEEK reported, "The Iranian crisis and the freezing of Iranian assets have Europeans frightened about what will come next. 'The dollar is like a hot potato,' says Freidrich W. Menzel, managing director of Citibank in Frankfurt."

The Europeans' fears about the Carter administration's economic mistakes were soon fulfilled. Just when it appeared things could not get worse, they did. On December 24, Soviet troops marched into Afghanistan, and eleven days later the Carter administration levied the **grain embargo**.

Uncle Eric

7

The Grain Embargo

Dear Chris,

In retaliation for the invasion of Afghanistan, the Carter administration prohibited American farmers from selling grain to the **Soviet Union.**[14] Mr. Carter threatened additional grave consequences if the Soviet troops did not immediately withdraw.

The theory was that these pressures would cause the Soviets to leave Afghanistan, stability would be restored. But the application was not quite so neat as the theory.

The embargo and accompanying vague threats blew the lid off the currency markets. Around the world, people began to fear that U.S. officials would pressure their allies into freezing all **Soviet Bloc**[15] assets.

At that time, Soviet Bloc debt to western banks totaled some $80 billion. Knowledgeable investors began to realize

---

[14] The Soviet government was a long-time enemy of the U.S. government. The Soviet Union included the countries of Russia, Estonia, Latvia, Lithuania, Belarus, Ukraine, Moldova, Georgia, Armenia, Azerbaijan, Kazakhstan, Uzbekistan, Turkmenistan, Tajikistan and Kirgizstan.

[15] The Soviet Bloc was the Soviet Union plus the nations it controlled. This was a huge area, about one-sixth of all the land on earth.

that if Soviet Bloc assets were frozen, the Soviet Bloc governments would be unable or unwilling to repay this debt.

With financial markets already in turmoil, an $80 billion default hitting dozens of large banks world-wide could set off a global bank run and financial crash every bit as bad as 1929.

Investors were also aware that each government would be tempted to try to bail out its banks by rapidly printing money and giving this money to the banks — by hyperinflating.

All banks and currencies everywhere were now threatened by Mr. Carter's actions, no paper money of any type was trusted. The demand for all paper money plunged and the demand for gold and silver skyrocketed.

Gold During the 1979—'80 Panic

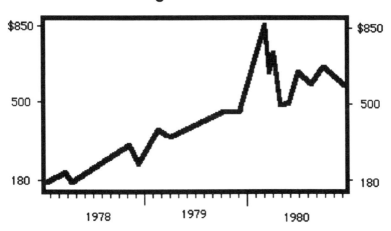

On January 31, 1980 the WALL STREET JOURNAL quoted Hans Baer, chairman of Bank Julius Baer in Switzerland: "Put bluntly, the main reason for the gold-price explosion is the Iranian assets freeze. And after Afghanistan, people fear that there could be some joint assets freeze by NATO. This leaves only gold and silver. This panic carries a latent danger of a loss of confidence in the entire system."

Day after day the financial panic grew. The demand for paper money plunged. Gold rose to $850 and silver to $50.

But few people understood what was happening because few understood velocity or the demand for money. Most news people had their gaze fixed firmly on the supply of money, and since this supply was not increasing rapidly, they assumed the exploding gold and silver prices were an **anomaly**.[16]

The Fed did the only thing it could do. To offset the declining demand for the dollar it tightened monetary policy, stopping expansion of the money supply.

Then it tightened further, triggering a **deflation**. The tightening was reinforced by credit controls restricting the flow of money. Interest rates rose three full points in one month.

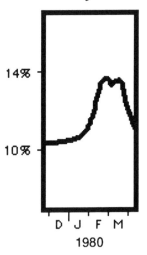

5-Year Treasury Security Rates

To restore confidence in the dollar and stop the panicky flight from dollars, the Federal Reserve restricted the money supply. This drove interest rates up three full points in one month.

---

16 A strange exception to what would be expected.

Officials held their breaths and waited. And waited. Finally the panic began to subside and precious metals prices broke downward.

After a few weeks had passed, investors lost their fear that the Carter administration would freeze Soviet Bloc assets. The perceived risk of holding bank deposits and paper money began to decline, and the demand for paper money began to stabilize. Interest rates fell back.

By May of 1980 the panic was over and paper money was again trusted — to some extent. As the LONDON TIMES wrote, investors in any given country now understand gold is an asset "no other government can inflate and no other government can block." And, as BUSINESS WEEK said, foreign bankers "will neither forgive nor forget" the panic of 1980.

Restoring confidence in the dollar would take a long, long time.

Uncle Eric

8

Ramifications of
the Panic of 1980

Dear Chris,

For several weeks in 1979-80 the world was approaching a financial catastrophe more massive than any seen before. Stage three inflation was developing *worldwide* and there was danger all paper money would become worthless, destroyed not by skyrocketing supply but by plummeting demand.

But this catastrophe did not materialize, and the most important reason may be that we were lucky. Wealthy Arabs who had invested their money in America were as unsophisticated about velocity as almost everyone else. In 1979 much of their American holdings were in the form of **illiquid** long-term investments such as real estate.

These investments could not be dumped on a moment's notice the way bank accounts and other **liquid** investments could. So, no matter how frightened these Arab investors were in 1980, they could not bail out. This kept the crisis from being as bad as it could have been, and eased the government's job of cooling the panic.

However, the wealthy Arabs learned much from the 1980 crisis. Writing in the March 23, 1984 WALL STREET JOURNAL, reporter Michael Seist pointed out that these Arabs had changed the way they invest. "Many long-term investments, such as real estate and long-term government securities," Mr. Seist said, "are being turned into short-term investments like bank deposits." He also pointed out that, "Being highly liquid will make it that much easier for the Arabs to sell off their dollar portfolios" in the future.

Remember, this was *four years* after the panic. Wealthy foreign investors were still nervous and ready to bail out of dollars.

Uncle Eric

9

The Gloom-and-Doomers

Dear Chris,

Another of the fascinating aspects of the 1980 panic concerns the reactions of the so-called gloom-and-doomers. During the 1970s many financial experts had been acquiring the reputation for being gloom-and-doomers because they had been predicting a runaway inflation and economic catastrophe. Their predictions were based on the assumption money supply would skyrocket.

In 1980, money supply was not skyrocketing. It was increasing significantly but certainly not enough to cause a **hyperinflation**. Some gloom-and-doomers concluded that the soaring gold and silver prices were an anomaly unjustified by prevailing economic conditions.

Even today I occasionally see an article that mentions the "fact" that gold and silver prices of 1980 were simply "too high" or "at ridiculous levels." The writers are apparently assuming the demand for money is not an important factor. If money supply is not exploding upward, then there is nothing to cause the dollar to crash, they seem to believe.

But as we have seen, in 1980 the demand for money became more important than money supply, and I see no reason to assume this condition has changed.

Fed officials have quite a bit of control over money supply, but almost none over the demand for money. The demand for money is a wild card, when it changes, all bets are off.

Uncle Eric

10

Two Important Questions

Dear Chris,

Perhaps the two most important questions to be asked about the Panic of 1980 are, how much did the politicians learn from their mistakes and how many of these politicians are still in the government today? The answers are, unfortunately, not much and not many.

The reason for the not much is simple. A politician does not get elected by understanding economics, finance, law, foreign affairs or the other important subjects about which he makes daily decisions. He gets elected by understanding how to get elected. That's what a politician is, a person who is an expert at winning elections. Expecting politicians to make wise decisions about things they know little about is unrealistic to say the least.

It is hardly an accident that for eight years the most popular president of the most powerful government on earth was a professional actor.[17] Since the days of ancient Greece, politics has been show business — the art of illusion — and it has attracted the types of people who are specialists in this.

---

[17] Ronald Reagan.

So, once in power, few politicians are equipped to understand what they are doing with their power. This was painfully obvious in 1980.

It seems likely that many who participated in the 1979-80 mistakes that caused the demand for money to plummet and velocity to skyrocket are still quite hazy about what velocity and the demand for money really are. Before 1979 they probably did not even realize such forces existed.

But even if they did learn from their mistakes, few of them are still around and those who are have no intention of publicizing their mistakes. Today the federal government is ruled by an entirely different set of politicians, most of whom are very likely as ignorant as their predecessors.

This was already clear in 1985 when President Reagan revealed he was considering freezing Nicaraguan assets. The mere fact that the president would *talk* about another freeze could have frightened enough foreign investors to trigger a plunge in the demand for dollars and a repeat of 1980. The panic didn't happen — Nicaragua was apparently seen by Arabs and other foreign investors as a special case unrelated to them — but the fact that Reagan was willing to take the risk tells us that little was learned from the 1980 debacle.

Indeed, it is quite possible that today's politicians not only did not learn crucial lessons from the 1980 crisis, they may have learned lessons that are wrong. They may understand so little about 1980, and about velocity and the demand for money, that they think Mr. Carter got away with it. So they may think they can, too. This is why it is important to be aware of what I call the financial hair-trigger, which I will introduce in the next letter.

Chris, I'd like to cite an example from the 1990s that demonstrates little was learned from the 1980 panic.

The stock market. To end the 1982 recession, Federal Reserve officials injected tens of billions of dollars into the economy. To stop the 1987 crash and 1991 recession, they injected tens of billions more, and they did not stop.

By 1997, the market had become the largest bubble in the history of the world.[18] A feeding frenzy developed as thousands of investors who knew almost nothing about stocks or mutual funds bought and sold them like gambling addicts in a casino. The velocity of the money in the stock market is hard to measure with much accuracy, but any knowledgeable observer could see it must have been very high.

One way to measure velocity in the stock market is to look at the number of shares traded. Here are figures for the New York Stock Exchange.

Shares Traded on the New York Stock Exchange
In Millions

1980	1985	1990	1995
11,562	27,774	39,946	87,873

Another way is to look at the value of the shares traded.

Value of Shares Traded on the New York Stock Exchange
In Billions of Dollars

1980	1985	1990	1995
$382	$981	$1,336	$3,110

---

[18] Largest in terms of the number of people and amount of money involved. A bubble is an economic hot spot created by the inflow of huge amounts of money. The stock market in the 1920s is the textbook example.

A completely accurate picture of velocity and the demand for money is never possible, but clearly, carloads of money were sloshing around in the stock market, changing hands at a furious pace.

Uncle Eric

11

The Financial Hair-Trigger

Dear Chris,

In a free economy, change tends to be an evolutionary[19] process and you can plan ahead. In a government-controlled economy, change tends to be a revolutionary process,[20] and you cannot plan ahead.

The evidence seems to show that velocity and the demand for money are not serious problems in a free economy. In the absence of **fiat**[21] **money** and **fiat law**, people have the ability to work, save and invest without fear that the government will suddenly change the rules. Being able to plan ahead, they feel secure and are not inclined to panic. I know of no case in all of history when people panicked to bail out of cash when the cash was gold or silver.

But in a government-controlled economy like ours, many major changes are caused, not by the masses of the people through gradual market mechanisms, but by politicians and

---

[19] The word evolution here has nothing to do with Darwin. It means slow and gradual.

[20] Rapid, sudden.

[21] Something easily done or undone at the whim of authorities. Whimsical. Quantities of fiat money are easily changed.

bureaucrats in the centers of power. These politicians and bureaucrats are human and they change their minds. They occasionally cause massive, instantaneous reversals in economic trends. The '79 freeze was only one of history's many electrifying examples. Another was the 1930 Smoot-Hawley tariffs which turned a recession into the Great Depression. In 1987, the Fed's tightening of monetary policy drove interest rates up and triggered a huge stock market crash.

The 1980 crisis was so widespread that wealthy individuals and organizations around the world learned unforgettable lessons about the insecurity inherent in a government-controlled economy. Like the wealthy Arabs in 1984, they are now much more uncomfortable being invested long-term.

This means a much larger portion of the money in the world is now what bankers call **hot money.** Its owners are quick to bail out if they catch the scent of trouble.

Thus the world financial system now has a financial hair-trigger. Millions of people are constantly alert and very sensitive to the slightest hint of change in government policy.

In other words, today any long-term plan is extremely risky. At any time, some politician or bureaucrat somewhere could utter an off-hand remark or casually suggest a strange new policy that could scare enough people to pull the hair-trigger and start the stampede. You could be caught unprepared, as the Arabs were in 1980, helplessly watching the security and value of your business and investments — your whole way of life — rapidly undermined.

This is what happened to your parents. Your father's real estate business flourished in the 1970s when interest rates were low. People could easily borrow the money to buy homes and other types of real estate.

Then U.S. officials froze Iranian assets, starting the great panic, and the Soviet invasion of Afghanistan poured gasoline on the fire. The only way the Federal Reserve could stop the panic was by restricting the money supply to offset the decline in the demand for money. This pushed **interest** rates[22] very high, and triggered the back-to-back 1980 and 1982 recessions. Your father's business was destroyed — by events on the other side. of the world. Like most Americans, your parents didn't even know where Iran or Afghanistan were, and they'd never heard of the Shah. I know this is hard to believe in light of current events, but eighteen years ago, few Americans could have pointed to Iran or Afghanistan on a map.

At that time, most teachers and textbooks, not unlike today, failed to explain how events on the other side of the world could affect your parents in their own home town. So your parents, like most Americans, had a tunnel-vision view of the economy. They looked no further than their own country. Some looked no further than their own home town.

An example of how quickly panic can be generated and the demand for money can plunge in a government-controlled economy appeared in Argentina in the summer of 1985. When *rumors* began circulating that Argentine politicians were *thinking* of freezing prices and issuing a new currency, merchants jacked up prices overnight, some by 75 percent or more. Shoppers roared through the supermarkets sweeping goods from the shelves, and in two days of frantic

---

22 Interest is the price of renting money. When the supply of money is restricted, the price rises.

black-market trading, the peso plunged 50 percent. On rumors!

The moral of the story is: In a government-controlled economy, short-term plans are the only kind that involve reasonable risks. They enable you to shift gears quickly if trouble begins to develop. Long-term plans are invitations to financial suicide.

The great crash of 1987 was an object lesson about the financial hair-trigger. When the stock market began to plunge, the panic spread world-wide within hours. A deflationary catastrophe like the 1930's Great Depression was averted only by the Federal Reserve's solemn promise to inject however much money into the banking system as was necessary to stop the crash.

At the end of the decade the world's central bankers remained fearful, the lessons of the 1980 panic and 1987 crash had not been forgotten:

"In the late 1970s the Carter administration and the IMF [International Monetary Fund] sold over 3,000 tons of gold in an attempt to wean central bankers off the metal. ... But old habits die hard. The inflationary surge of 1979-81 made central bankers seek refuge in the traditional haven of gold. Even though inflation and gold prices have since fallen, the buying goes on. In seven of the past nine years central banks have been net buyers of gold, adding 983 tons to their holdings."

— THE ECONOMIST, 8/19/89, p. 61

Uncle Eric

12

Federal Reserve Behavior

Dear Chris,

Some years ago in testimony before Congress, Federal Reserve Chairman Paul Volcker was asked what the Fed was going to do next. Mr. Volcker admitted, "I don't know what the Federal Reserve is going to do next."[23]

The Fed has a serious problem, it does not know how to conduct monetary policy. How could it? There is no reasonable way to decide what to do with the supply of money when we do not know what the demand for money will be.

The demand for money is very difficult to measure with much accuracy and it is impossible to **forecast**. Velocity calculations are of only slight help because they are so rough. The most commonly used measure is to divide **Gross National Product (GNP)** by the money supply to determine how many times the average dollar changed hands to make the production possible. In recent years this has run in the neighborhood of six to seven times.

---

[23] WALL STREET JOURNAL, March 19, 1985.

But in any given month or quarter, the calculations typically show wild swings of as much as plus or minus five percent, sometimes more.

If these calculations were accurate they would be terrifying. A five percent increase in velocity is the equivalent of a five percent increase in the money supply — in one month!

The velocity calculations are useful only over very long time spans. When they are averaged over five or ten years they show rather distinct trends. But anyone who promises greater precision than this has either discovered an amazing new technique of measurement or is selling snake oil.

Velocity Statistics Are Erratic

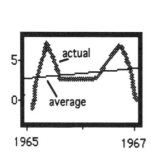

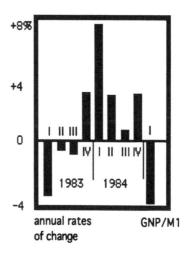

Velocity statistics swing wildly from quarter to quarter. The years 1965-67 and 1983-84 were typical. A reasonably clear picture emerges only when the statistics are averaged over many years.

Other measures are sometimes used — the number of checks passing through the banks, for instance — but nothing has been found that is very accurate. Each individual makes daily buy and sell decisions depending on how he or she feels about the need for cash versus the need for goods or services. Tracking the attitudes of millions of people is simply impossible, and will probably remain so forever. We all have free wills and change our minds frequently.

So, the Fed must decide what the money supply will be without having the slightest idea what the demand for money will be. Throughout 1984, for instance, velocity was rising (see chart). In the fourth quarter it registered a near four percent annual rate of increase. Then in the first quarter of 1985 it made a complete reversal, falling at a four percent rate. If you were the Fed, what would you have done, tighten to offset the established rising trend or loosen to offset the new falling trend?

In making your decision you would have had to keep four points in mind. First, you probably cannot know what velocity will be doing at the time you will be inflating or deflating. This can be seen by the fact that the 1980 crisis was so short-lived it has never shown up in the velocity statistics even though bankers and precious metals dealers worldwide were watching it happen all around them. Talk with some who are old enough to remember and you will hear that on every continent, investors were in a panic to get rid of their paper currencies and get into precious metals. The Federal Reserve was having historic emergency meetings to begin the tight money measures to combat the crisis, and the statistics never have shown the crisis even happened.

Second, if you inflated the money supply at, say, a 15 percent rate, at a time when velocity was rising at, say, 15 percent, then you would actually have been "pumping the accelerator" at 30 percent. *Without realizing it,* you would be flirting with another monetary disaster because 30 percent would certainly trigger a flight from the dollar if it continued very long.

Third, it is much easier to stop a deflation than an inflation. You can always print a few tons of money and pass it around to stop a deflation but once inflation is into stage three, your hands are tied and catastrophe is all but certain.

Fourth, recessions usually bring a cooling of velocity. They create a climate of fear which causes people to hoard cash.

So, you are a navigator without charts or compass, what do you do?

My guess is you would err on the side of caution. You would stay tight enough to keep the economy in a perpetual recession so that you could be sure you were not inflating too heavily. Staying in a recession would be the only way you could be confident you were not about to pull the financial hair-trigger and launch a hyperinflation.

In short, a recession would be your only reliable indicator that velocity was under control.

So, I believe this is why the 1980's recovery was a myth and why unemployment, poverty and bankruptcies remained widespread. Federal officials had no choice but to keep the money supply tight, and the economy in a recession, until they were certain they had restored confidence in the dollar. My guess is it took ten years to do that, and your family was one of the victims.

In 1997, U.S. officials came out with a new way to track velocity and the demand for money. They now offer an "inflation-indexed" [24] **bond**. These new bonds pay interest that is tied to the **consumer price index** (CPI). When the CPI rises, the bond's interest rises, too.

The government's other bonds do not have this feature, their rates of interest are fixed. So, when investors are getting nervous about the value of the dollar, the other bonds will not be as appealing as the new indexed bonds.

Officials will track the difference in demand between other bonds and indexed bonds, and when they see the other bonds losing favor to the indexed bonds they'll know investors are getting worried about the stability of the dollar.

Chris, I suggest you track the bonds yourself, the WALL STREET JOURNAL and other financial publications report on them. A sharp increase in demand for "inflation-indexed" bonds over other bonds can be taken as an indicator that the demand for money is falling and velocity rising. The Fed will need to tighten the money supply and raise interest rates to restore confidence in the dollar. This will almost certainly mean a recession, or at least a slowdown, and a deflation of whatever hot spots exist at the time. If you are in one of these hot spots, this will be crucial information for you.

Mark this page and refer back to it after you have finished reading my future set of letters about hot spots.[25] These new bonds will be very important to you, Chris.

Uncle Eric

---

24 An IOU.

25 See THE CLIPPER SHIP STRATEGY by Richard Maybury, published by Bluestocking Press, Placerville, CA.

13

Another Important Lesson

Dear Chris,

From the Iranian assets freeze we learn another important lesson: Have an international outlook. What the U.S. government does on the other side of the world often affects you and your family more than what it does in your home town.

In fact, the government's foreign policy can completely overwhelm events at home. Aside from the Panic of 1980, we also have the example of the Vietnam War. To finance it, the government created tens of billions of dollars and plunged us into the inflationary chaos of the 1970s.

The 1973 Arab-Israeli War is a further example. The U.S. government's support of the Israeli government angered the Arab oil producers. The result was the Arab oil embargo, soaring oil prices, the "energy crisis" and the bankruptcies of thousands of firms.

The 1990 Iraqi invasion of Kuwait caused another crisis. The oil price doubled to $40 per barrel and the stock market dropped 19 percent.

In short, the world has been unified economically. Our transportation and communication systems are now so effective that all mankind lives in a single global economy.

But the governments do not like this, they fight it. They greedily cling to their borders, tariffs and other artificial boundaries that should have vanished with the coming of the telephone and radio. This primitive behavior creates great risk for business people and investors, as governments continue to fight over territory.[26]

Chris, a good research project is to go back through history and find more examples of events abroad affecting Americans at home. Americans do not have a tradition of watching events in foreign nations so they are often **blindsided**.[27] This creates an advantage for investors who do watch international events.

Uncle Eric

---

[26] This should not be taken as an endorsement for one world government. Far from it. It is simply the recognition that the world has already been unified economically and governments don't like it.

[27] A football term meaning to be hit from one direction while looking in the other direction.

14

The Lesson of the '87 Crash

Dear Chris,

Years after the 1987 stock market crash we are still debating what it all means. I have two thoughts about it. The first is simply that the crash was proof the financial hair-trigger exists and is very touchy. Eight years after the panic of 1980, millions of investors around the world were still nervous and ready to bail out fast, and I see no reason to think this has changed.

The second thought is a bit more complex. The conventional view of the government's monetary policy is that officials try to inflate the money supply at a rate that will keep us in a safe zone between inflationary boom and deflationary bust. If they print too little money we get a recession and if they print too much we get a **double-digit inflation**.

This assumption that the lines are parallel is based on lack of understanding of the causes of business cycles. As explained in my seventh letter on economics,[28] when officials inject money into the economy, this causes business people to

---

[28] See chapter seven in "Wallpaper, Wheelbarrows and Recessions" in WHATEVER HAPPENED TO PENNY CANDY? by Richard J. Maybury, published by Bluestocking Press, Placerville, CA.

CONVENTIONAL VIEW
Federal Reserve Monetary Policy

The widespread assumption is that the Federal Reserve attempts to keep its monetary policy (rate of inflation of the money supply) running in a safe zone between parallel areas of boom and bust.

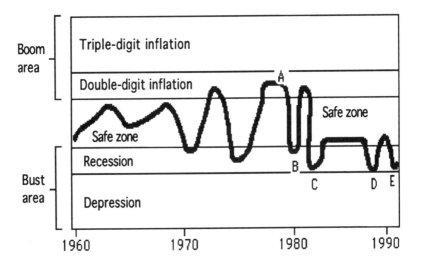

◣◣◣◣ Federal Reserve monetary policy.

A   Heavy inflation in late 1970s.

B   Mild recession in 1980. Inflation did not stop.

C   1982 recession was worst since Great Depression.
        Inflation reduced.

D   1987 stock crash was worst since Great Depression.

E   1991 recession. Inflation reduced.

make mistakes. Firms are created and expanded, and employees are hired, in areas where they would not otherwise be — meaning in areas where the new money is appearing — and these firms and employees are then dependent on a continued flow of this money. If officials stop expanding the money supply, these firms and employees go broke. This disorganization of firms and employees is called the "injection effect."

Chris, I'll discuss the injection effect in a later set of letters. It is crucially important for you to understand. If your parents had understood it in the 1980s they would have stood a better chance of weathering the storm. They do understand now, and plan all their business and investment decisions based on what I call the Clipper Ship Strategy.

Each injection of new money causes more disorganization of firms and employees, which means *the effects are cumulative.* Every year more people become dependent on the continued flow of newly printed money. In 1950, an injection of $10 billion stopped the recession; in 1983, $100 billion was needed; in 1993, $350 billion. An unknown but certainly large portion of that $350 billion ended up sloshing around in the stock market.

Because each injection causes more disorganization, the economy becomes more fragile. This is the lesson of the 1980 panic, the 1982 recession and the 1987 stock crash. We are living in a crystal vase that cracks easily and may shatter. The vase is beautiful but delicate. The 1987 tightening of monetary policy was not at all severe but it brought the worst stock market crash since 1929. Ever since, the Fed has been reluctant to tighten the money supply very much, which is why the stock market skyrocketed well above 7,000 in 1997.

Combine all this disorganization of firms and employees with the financial-hair trigger that could cause velocity to soar and we get this picture of monetary policy.

MORE REALISTIC VIEW
Federal Reserve Monetary Policy

The lines between boom and bust are not parallel, they are converging. The safe zone is narrowing because each injection of new money causes more disorganization of businesses; the economy is becoming more fragile.

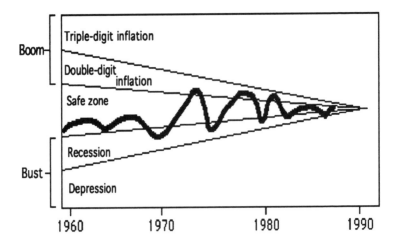

The illustration is a theoretical model, not a forecast. It is meant only to give you a mental picture of what is happening. I do not know if the 1990s will be the decade when our luck runs out. Maybe we will make it into the next century, maybe not. We might even make it to the year 2010 or 2020 without a major catastrophe, there is simply no way to know. Neither the extent of the disorganization nor the Fed's behavior are measurable or predictable.

I do not want to give the impression I am certain this view is correct. There isn't much in economics that we can be certain about, it's a young science. I am only saying that this picture seems to me to agree with the evidence better than the conventional picture does.

I am sure that we've seen this model at work in France, Argentina, Brazil, Mexico, Germany and many other nations. Each injection of new money caused more disorganization and more fragility, until officials finally went a bit too far in one direction or the other and triggered a runaway inflation or depression.

Chris, another research project for you would be to check into the runaway inflations and subsequent depressions that hit those countries. History does repeat.

You will find these economic crises almost always bring political upheaval. One of the most dramatic and well documented cases in history was Russia in the 1990s. I suggest you research that one first, it's so typical you can take it as a model for the others.

In fact, after you research 1990s Russia, go back and research the great panic of 1979-80, especially the emergency meetings at the Federal Reserve. Knowing what happened in Russia you will be able to see what federal officials were trying to avert in 1979-80.

Uncle Eric

15

What You Can Do About It

Dear Chris,

In planning your business and investment future, keep the following in mind: We cannot know what will happen next, so make plans accordingly. Keep all your time horizons short. *Don't get into anything you can't get out of fast.*

For your investments, do what central bankers do, own some gold and silver. Ten percent of your liquid assets in gold and silver coins is good insurance.

I believe these inflation hedges will stay down and perhaps even decline — or at least I hope so — as long as the dollar remains trusted. But sooner or later officials will make another mistake that will cause the demand for money to fall and velocity to soar, and when this happens we may not be as lucky as in 1980. This time the panic may not stop. If it doesn't, I would expect the precious metals to triple or quadruple within weeks.

U.S. government Treasury Bills are an excellent protection against deflation. I always have a lot of those, but they require a minimum investment of $2500 (via a Treasury Bill money market mutual fund). Until you accumulate that much savings, I suggest you put your money in U.S. Savings

Bonds which you can get for as little as $25.00. Savings Bonds are equally good protection against deflation.

In your career or business, be flexible and ready to make changes at any moment. I will explain that in great detail in a future set of letters.[29]

We saw a lot of history unfold during the 1980s and this was only the beginning. We will encounter many dangers and many opportunities, be ready for anything, and spread the word.

Uncle Eric

---

[29] See THE CLIPPER SHIP STRATEGY by Richard Maybury, published by Bluestocking Press, Placerville, CA.

Early Warning Symptoms

U.S. Treasury Secretary William Simon gave this testimony before the House Sub-Committee on Democratic Research Organization on April 30, 1976, just three years before the panic of 1979-80 began:

"In the case of the federal government, we can print money to pay for our folly for a time. But we will just continue to debase our currency, and then we will have financial collapse. This is the road we are on today. This is the direction in which the 'humanitarians' are leading us. But there is nothing 'humanitarian' about the collapse of a great industrial civilization. There is nothing 'humanitarian' about the panic, the chaos, the riots, the starvation, the death that will ensue. There is nothing 'humanitarian' about the dictatorship that must inevitably take over as terrified people cry out for leadership. There is nothing 'humanitarian' about the loss of freedom. That is why we must be concerned about the cancerous growth of government and its steady devouring of our citizens' productive energy. That is why we must be concerned about deficits and balancing the budget. The issue is not bookkeeping, it is not accounting. The issue is the liberty of the American people.

Forgive me, Mr. Chairman. I have not been addressing your specific questions. I just wanted to put the real issue in focus. I can speak to the technicalities, and I will do so. But they obscure the real issue that faces us in the country today. The problems of deficits, budget balancing, capital markets — all these are important. But it is more important, I think, to understand that these are just early warning symptoms of a disease that threatens the very life of our body politic. And if we continue to move down this same path, that disease will become irreversible, and our liberty will be lost. I speak of this so insistently because I hear no one discussing this danger. Congress does not discuss it. The press does not discuss it. Look around us — the press isn't even here! The people do not discuss it — they are unaware of it. No counterforce in America is being mobilized to fight this danger. The battle is being lost, and not a shot is being fired.

That, Mr. Chairman, is why for me the last few years in office have been like a bad dream. I am leaving Washington next January. I am going to go home to New Jersey a very frightened man."

— Treasury Secretary William Simon
April 30, 1976

When Mr. Simon gave this testimony, the U.S. money supply[30] was $300 billion. Within four years it was $400 billion, and today it is $1.1 trillion.

In 1980, we dodged a bullet. Will we be this lucky the next time?

---

[30] Measured by M1.

16

Summary

Dear Chris,

Here is a summary of the important points covered in this set of letters:

1. The economy is not a machine, it is people. When the government makes "adjustments" to the economy it is manipulating the businesses, careers and investments of innocent people.

2. Velocity and the demand for money are poorly understood and rarely discussed, but they are crucially important to us all.

3. History repeats. The French runaway inflation of the 1790s is filled with lessons for us today. Review the three stages of inflation so that you remember them well.

4. Economics is a young and very inexact science so we cannot be sure about very much. But it appears that

the great financial panic of 1980 was driven by rising velocity and the falling demand for money, not rising money supply.

5. The panic of 1980 was a demonstration of the fact that events in foreign countries can affect us more than events in our home towns. We should pay at least as much attention to the rest of the world as we do to our own country. (In a future set of letters I will help you get started by writing about THE THOUSAND YEAR WAR in the Middle East and how it affects us today.)[31]

6. In a free economy, change tends to be evolutionary. In a government-controlled economy, change tends to be revolutionary.

7. Velocity and the demand for money are extremely difficult to track. The new "inflation-indexed" bonds will be a big help.

8. For your investments, your long-term plan should be to have no long-term plan. We do not know what government officials will do, so don't get into anything you can't get out of fast, in a few days.

Chris, don't let the government's control over your future business, career and investments get you down. There is a lot of truth to those old clichés, knowledge is power, and forewarned is forearmed.

---

[31] See the forthcoming title THE THOUSAND YEAR WAR: THE LITTLE UNDERSTOOD MID-EAST CONFLICT AND HOW IT AFFECTS YOU TODAY by Richard Maybury, published by Bluestocking Press, Placerville, CA.

Having read this and my previous sets of letters, you know a great deal more about economics than most adults do, and you have a much better chance of protecting yourself and prospering. It's a great   head start. A future set of letters will give you lots of specific nuts-and-bolts how-to advice.[32]

Until then make it a habit to learn everything you can about business, economics and history, and encourage everyone you care about to do the same. It's not only fascinating, it is essential for achieving financial security.

Uncle Eric

Spread the Word!

---

[32] See THE CLIPPER SHIP STRATEGY by Richard Maybury, published by Bluestocking Press, Placerville, CA.

"Inflation is like sin; every government denounces it and every government practices it."

— Sir Frederick Keith-Ross (1887-1968)
quoted in THE OBSERVER, June 30, 1957

"The issuers may have, and in the case of government paper, always have, a direct interest in lowering the value of the currency, because it is the medium in which their own debts are computed."

— John Stuart Mill, (1806-1873)
Principles of Politifal Economy, ed. Ashley,
Bk.III, Ch. XIII,1,p.544

Please Write "Uncle Eric" With Your Ideas, Questions and Concerns

Watch for future books by Richard J. Maybury. One will be answers to questions from readers. Send your questions or comments to him in care of "Uncle Eric," Bluestocking Press, P.O. Box 1014, Dept. MM, Placerville, CA 95667-1014. All letters become property of Bluestocking Press and may be published in whole or in part without payment to the writer. Please tell us if you want your name kept confidential. Topics can include, but are not limited to economics, government, history and law.

If your letter is published in a future "Uncle Eric" book or used in a future "Uncle Eric" audiocassette tape you will receive a free autographed copy of that book or tape.

Bibliography

- FIAT MONEY INFLATION IN FRANCE by Andrew Dickson White, Foundation for Economic Education, Irvington-on-Hudson, NY.

- THE GREAT INFLATION by William Guttmann and Patricia Meehan, Gordon & Cremonesi, Great Britain, 1975, ISBN 0-86033-035-4.

- EXTRAORDINARY POPULAR DELUSIONS AND THE MADNESS OF CROWDS by Charles Mackay, LL.D., Harmony Books, NY 1980.

Mail Order Bookstores

Bluestocking Press, P.O. Box 1014, Dept. MM, Placerville, CA 95667, 1-800-959-8586.

Foundation for Economic Education, Irvington-on-Hudson, NY 10533.

Henry-Madison Research, Box 1616 V, Rocklin, CA 95677.

Laissez Faire Books, 942 Howard St., San Francisco, CA 94103.

The Liberator Catalog, Advocates for Self-Government, 3955 Pleasantdale Road #106A, Atlanta, GA 30340.

Liberty Tree Network, 134 98th Avenue, Oakland, CA 94603.

**Contact your librarian or a used bookstore
for locating out-of-print books.**

Glossary

ANOMALY. A strange exception to what would be expected.

ASSIGNAT. French paper money.

BLACK MARKET. The production, sale or trade of goods or services against the wishes of the government. Example: Liquor was a black market product during the "Prohibition Era."

BLIND-SIDED. A football term meaning to be hit from one direction while looking in the other direction.

BOND. An IOU. Bond usually means a long-term IOU — several years or decades, not months.

BUSINESS CYCLE. The boom/bust cycle. Prosperity followed by recession followed by prosperity followed by recession, and so forth.

CONSUMER PRICE INDEX. The U.S. government's estimate of the overall price level of goods purchased by consumers.

COUP D' ETAT. Violent overthrow of the government by a small group of individuals.

DEFLATION. Commonly used to mean a decrease in prices. Actually a decrease in the amount of money, which causes a decrease in prices. Also usually causes depressions and falling prices.

DEMAND FOR MONEY. The desire to hold money rather than trade it away. High demand for money means money is traded away reluctantly. Low demand for money means money is traded away quickly.

DEPRESSION. The correction period following an inflation. Usually includes a lot of business failures and unemployment.

DICTATOR. Someone who rules with absolute, arbitrary power and control.

DOUBLE-DIGIT INFLATION. Price increases rising at 10 to 99 percent per year due to inflation.

ECONOMICS. The study of the production and distribution of wealth (goods and services).

FED. See Federal Reserve.

FEDERAL RESERVE. The central bank of the U.S. Controls the supply of money and attempts to control interest rates.

FIAT. Something easily done or undone at the whim of authorities. Whimsical.

FIAT LAW. Law not logically derived from ethical principles. Law made up by lawmakers according to the rule: whatever appears necessary.

FIAT MONEY. Money created by a legal tender law. Money not backed by gold or silver.

FIRST STAGE INFLATION. In the first stage, prices do not rise as fast as the money supply does because people don't understand what is happening. Some delay their spending in hopes prices will fall back. In effect, they take some of the money out of circulation as the government is pumping it in. This was France in 1790.

FORECAST. Predict.

FREEZE. To hold in place. In economics, "freeze" is usually used in reference to prices or supplies of goods. A government can forbid traders to change their prices, or forbid them to sell or transport their goods.

GNP. See Gross National Product.

GRAIN EMBARGO. A law forbidding farmers to sell grain to certain buyers.

GROSS NATIONAL PRODUCT. The government's estimate of the production of finished goods and services.

HOT MONEY. Money changing hands quickly.

HYPERINFLATION. An inflation in which prices are rising at triple-digit (or more) rates per year.

ILLIQUID. Not easily sold or traded. Real estate is illiquid compared to stocks, for instance.

INFLATION. Commonly used to mean an increase in prices. Actually an increase in the amount of money, which causes an increase in prices by reducing the value of each unit of money.

INJECTION EFFECT. The changes that occur on Wall Street (the financial world) and Main Street (where most of us live and work) when the government injects new money into the economy.

INTEREST. The price of renting money. When the supply of money is less than the demand, the interest rates rise.

LEGAL TENDER LAW. A law saying you will be punished if you do not accept a given type of money in trade for your goods or services.

LIQUID. Easily sold or traded.

MANDAT. The French paper money that replaced the assignat.

MONEY. The most easily traded thing in a society. Economists call it the most liquid commodity.

MONEY SUPPLY. The amount of money in a country or economy. In recent years economists have begun to try to measure the total world money supply as well as the money supplies of individual countries.

PAPER MONEY. Today usually means fiat money. Money created by legal tender laws.

POLITICAL POWER. The privilege of using force on persons who have not harmed anyone. The legal privilege of backing one's decisions with violence or threats of violence. Not the same thing as influence, which implies that a person has the option to walk away.

RUN. A sudden strong surge of buying or selling. Also, a panic, usually either by depositors to remove their money from a bank, or by holders of a currency or investment to quickly trade the currency or investment away. A "run on the dollar" would mean holders of dollars were in a panic to trade their dollars for something they value or trust more.

RUNAWAY INFLATION. A hyperinflation. Prices rising rapidly.

SECOND STAGE INFLATION. In the second stage, many people have begun to understand what is happening, and are spending their money quickly. Prices rise faster than the money supply because each unit of the money is changing hands fast, making more transactions possible. Wanting to get rid of it fast, many are willing to accept less for it.

SOVIET BLOC. The Soviet Bloc was the Soviet Empire — the Soviet Union plus the nations it controlled. This was a huge area, about one-sixth of all the land on earth.

SOVIET UNION. The Soviet government was a long-time enemy of the U.S. government. The Soviet Union was made of the countries of Russia, Estonia, Latvia, Lithuania, Belarus, Ukraine, Moldova, Georgia, Armenia, Azerbaijan, Kazakhstan, Uzbekistan, Turkmenistan, Tajikistan and Kirgizstan.

THIRD STAGE INFLATION. In the third stage (the runaway) the whole population is in a panic to get rid of the money as soon as they get their hands on it, and the money declines to its real value, which is the value of scrap paper.

VELOCITY. The speed at which money changes hands. A measure of the demand for money.

About Richard J. Maybury "Uncle Eric"

Richard J. Maybury, also known as "Uncle Eric," is the former Global Affairs editor of Moneyworld, and widely regarded as one of the top free-market writers in America. His articles have appeared in the Wall Street Journal, USA Today and other major publications.

He's been a consultant to business firms in the U.S. and Europe. He is president of Henry-Madison Research.

His books have been endorsed by top business leaders including former U.S. Treasury Secretary William Simon, and he has been interviewed on more than 200 radio and TV shows across America.

He has authored eight books in the "Uncle Eric" series and writes an investment newsletter.

He has lived abroad, been around the world, and visited 48 states and 26 countries.

He is a teacher for all ages.

Index

Here's what reviewers have to say about prior editions of Richard J.Maybury's WHATEVER HAPPENED TO PENNY CANDY?

From the International World of Economics
"Must reading for anyone who wishes to understand the basics of our free enterprise system." —William E. Simon
Former U.S. Secretary of the Treasury

"This book is must reading for children of all ages. It's presentation of some of the fundamentals of economics is lucid, accurate and above all highly readable."
—Michael A. Walker, Executive Director
The Fraser Institute, British Columbia, Canada

From the World of Finance and Investment
"Probably the best short course in economics around and is more valuable than a college text that's ten times its length. Buy a dozen and give them to friends. This is a great book!"
—Douglas Casey, Author
Crisis Investing and *Strategic Investing*

"Maybury's book is a valuable contribution to economic literacy. It should be required reading for every student. Buy at least two copies of WHATEVER HAPPENED TO PENNY CANDY: one for you and your family; one as a gift for a member of Congress!"
—Jean Ross Peterson, Author
It Doesn't Grow on Trees

"One of the best books I've read explains the process (of government growth and inflation) very easily — especially for people that would like a good introduction to economics. It's also a great book to present to your youngsters."
— Joe Bradley, *Investor's Hotline*

From Entrepreneurs
"You'll find yourself saying "Ah...so!" more than once as you breeze through this delightful book, and you'll be looking for someone to share it with as soon as you've finished it."
— Barbara Brabec, Editor
National Home Business Report

Here's what reviewers have to say about Richard J.Maybury's WHATEVER HAPPENED TO JUSTICE?

From the International World of Economics

"This is a wonderfully readable and interesting book about the legal principles which undergird a free society. Richard Maybury challenges the reader to explore the inextricable connections between law and economics, and between economic and political liberty. I can think of no more important subject, and I highly recommend this lucid and thoughtful volume." —**William E. Simon**
Former U.S. Treasury Secretary and President, John M. Olin Foundation

From Legislators

"Richard Maybury's *Whatever Happened to Justice?* is critical reading for all Americans. If our economic and political downfall is to be avoided, we must expose an entire generation of Americans to the ideas found in this wonderful book."
—**Ron Paul, former member of Congress**

"Mr. Maybury has done an outstanding job of reminding us of the origin of common law and its vital importance to the preservation of freedom." —**Don Rogers**
California State Senator

From the Legal World

"Every lawyer should wonder "Whatever Happened to Justice?" Maybury's book indicts statism in our courtrooms and renders a verdict of guilty beyond any reasonable doubt. His work is a Corpus Juris Naturalis!"
—**Ellis Rexwood Curry, IV**
Attorney at Law

From the World of Education

"There is a naked clarity to Maybury's thought that washes over the reader like cleansing rain. His examination of the dynamics of common law is brilliant. As a teacher for all ages, Mr. Maybury is a virtuoso. Bravo!"
—**John Taylor Gatto**
former New York State Teacher of the Year and 3X New York City Teacher of the Year.
author of DUMBING US DOWN

From the World of Homeschooling

"Maybury has a gift for translating what sounds like tedious information into very personalized examples.....No matter what else you use, this book is a must! Highly recommended for reading and discussion. "

—Cathy Duffy, Author
CHRISTIAN HOME EDUCATORS' CURRICULUM MANUAL

From the World of Finance and Investment

"Unless we return to the principles of common and natural law, America is headed for totalitarianism. Richard Maybury's book will bring us back from the brink, and restore freedom and responsibility to this great nation."

—Mark Skousen, editor of FORECASTS & STRATEGIES

"Richard Maybury is one of my favorite people. All of his writing is clear and direct. Most important — it's philosophically uncompromising. If you want» the answers to how a truly free society would solve the problems of poverty, pollution, drugs, consumer proection, and the like, this book has them. If you're looking for a worthwhile gift for a young person especially, give this book."

—Doug Casey
editor of CRISIS INVESTING

From Authors

"We are drowning in an ocean of crazy laws and litigation. This book is a life preserver, a reminder of the fundamental rules which are needed for a free society."

—Karl Hess
author of CAPITALISM FOR KIDS
former U.S. Presidential speechwriter
former Associate Editor of NEWSWEEK

"WHATEVER HAPPENED TO JUSTICE? is an important book. Maybury explains how civilization depends on shared common values of right and wrong — how a revival of the Common Law would strengthen those values and reverse the destructive trends of modern society. The common sense approach of this book makes it an excellent tool for introducing these ideas to children."

—Philip Martin Koehne
President, KDF, Inc.
author of THE CULT OF LEGISLATION

Henry-Madison Research

Richard Maybury writes an investment newsletter about stocks, geopolitics, economics, bonds, currencies, real estate, interest rates, precious metals and more. Much analysis is based on the connection between law and economics. Mr. Maybury gives special attention to events in the former U.S.S.R. and Mideast, as well as in the U.S.

For a sample copy of Mr. Maybury's newsletter that gives you his latest thinking on important matters that affect you and your money send $5.00 to Henry-Madison Research, Box 1616-V, Rocklin, CA 95677.

For information about Mr. Maybury's lengthy special research reports send a self-addressed stamped business-size envelope to the above address.

Uncle Eric's Model
of How the World Works
quality paperbacks
Book 2:   ages 10 through adult
All other books: ages 14 through adult

Book 1. UNCLE ERIC TALKS ABOUT PERSONAL, CAREER & FINANCIAL SECURITY.
The Model introduced. Transcript of keynote speech. 45 pgs.

Book 2. WHATEVER HAPPENED TO PENNY CANDY?
The economic model explained. Quite simply the clearest
most interesting explanation of economics around. 124 pgs.

Book 3. WHATEVER HAPPENED TO JUSTICE?
The legal model explained. Explores America's legal heritage.
Discusses the difference between higher law and man-made
law, and the connection between rational law and economic
prosperity. Not to be missed. 256 pgs.

Book 4. ARE YOU LIBERAL? CONSERVATIVE? OR CONFUSED?
Political labels. What do they mean? Liberal, conservative,
left, right, democrat, republican, moderate, socialist, libertarian, communist—what are their economic policies and what
plans do their promoters have for your money? Clear, concise
explanations. Facts and fallacies. The model applied and
misapplied. 140 pgs.

Book 5. ANCIENT ROME: HOW IT AFFECTS YOU TODAY.
The model ignored. Are we heading for fascism like Ancient
Rome? Mr. Maybury uses historical events to explain current
events. Take a look at ancient Roman government and how it
affects you today. 92 pgs.

Book 6. EVALUATING BOOKS: WHAT WOULD THOMAS JEFFERSON THINK ABOUT
THIS? Learn to identify philosophical slants of most writers and
media commentators on the subjects of law, history, economics, and literature. 106 pgs.

Book 7. THE MONEY MYSTERY. Explains one of the least understood forces
that affect businesses, careers and investments. 90 pgs.

Book 8. THE CLIPPER SHIP STRATEGY. A practical nuts-and-bolts strategy for
prospering in our turbulent economy. 270 pgs.

Book 9. THE THOUSAND YEAR WAR —*forthcoming title.*

See order information on the following page.

Bluestocking Press

"Uncle Eric" Books by Richard J. Maybury

UNCLE ERIC TALKS ABOUT PERSONAL, CAREER & FINANCIAL SECURITY. . $ 7.95
WHATEVER HAPPENED TO PENNY CANDY? . . . . $ 9.95
WHATEVER HAPPENED TO JUSTICE? $14.95
ARE YOU LIBERAL? CONSERVATIVE? OR CONFUSED? . . . . $ 9.95
ANCIENT ROME: HOW IT AFFECTS YOU TODAY . . . . $ 8.95
EVALUATING BOOKS: WHAT WOULD THOMAS JEFFERSON
      THINK ABOUT THIS? . . . . $ 8.95
THE MONEY MYSTERY . . . . $ 8.95
THE CLIPPER SHIP STRATEGY $15.95
Uncle Eric's Model (SAVE! Includes eight books above) $77.00
THE THOUSAND YEAR WAR—*forthcoming title* . . . . query

Study Guides
Study Guides are available or forthcoming for all books listed above.
Contact publisher for price and availability.

Other Bluestocking Press Titles
HOW TO STOCK A HOME LIBRARY INEXPENSIVELY. $14.95
THE HOME SCHOOL MARKET GUIDE-7TH EDITION . . . . $158.00 postpaid
JONATHAN MAYHEW'S SERMON / JOHN ADAMS' EXPLANATION OF
      THE AMERICAN REVOLUTION. $4.95
LAURA INGALLS WILDER & ROSE WILDER LANE HISTORICAL TIMETABLE . . $2.00

> Prices subject to change without notice—confirm price with publisher
> before ordering. Phone 916-621-1123 • 800-959-8586 • Fax 916-642-9222

Order information: Order any of the above from Bluestocking Press (see address below). Payable in U.S. funds. If not postpaid, add shipping/handling as follows: First book, add $2.50 (book rate shipping) or $3.50 (foreign orders, surface shipping); each additional book: add $0.75. California residents add sales tax.

The Bluestocking Press Catalog targets preK through adults and specializes in American History, economics, law, and entrepreneurship. It also includes an excellent math program for ages 14 and up. History selections are arranged chronologically and include: Fiction, nonfiction, primary source material, historical documents, facsimile newspapers, historical music, historical toy-making kits, audio history, coloring books and more. Catalog free with book order. Otherwise for immediate first class shipping of the catalog please remit: U.S. addresses: $3.00. Foreign addresses: $3.00 surface shipping or $5.00 air shipping. Payable in U.S. funds to:

Bluestocking Press
P.O. Box 1014 • Dept. MM • Placerville • CA • 95667 • USA
Phone orders: 916-621-1123; 800-959-8586 (for MC / Visa orders)
FAX: 916-642-9222

The Money Mystery

*The
Hidden Force
Affecting Your
Career, Business
and Investments*

ASSIGNAT

MANDAT

MARK

*by
Richard J.
Maybury*